19

SHARKS

BY JOANNE MATTERN

BENCHMARK BOOKS

MARSHALL CAVENDISH
NEW YORK

Series Consultant:
James Doherty
General Curator
The Bronx Zoo, New York

Thank you to Paul L. Sieswerda, Curator, New York Aquarium, for his expert reading of this manuscript.

Benchmark Books
Marshall Cavendish Corporation
99 White Plains Road
Tarrytown, NY 10591–9001
Website: www.marshallcavendish.com

Library of Congress Cataloging–in–Publication Data
Mattern, Joanne
Sharks / by Joanne Mattern.
p. cm.–(Animals animals)
Includes bibliographical references and index.
ISBN 0-7614-1261-1
1. Sharks–Juvenile literature. [1. Sharks.] I. Title. II. Series.

QL638.9.M42 2001   597.3 21; aa05 11–20–dc00   00-052325

Cover photo: *Visuals Unlimited* © David B. Fleetham

All photographs are used by permission and through the courtesy of Visuals Unlimited, Inc.: © David B. Fleetham, 5, 15, 18 (center), 20; David Wrobel, 12 (bottom), 19 (bottom); Marty Snyderman,16; A. Kerstitch, 24. © Norbert Wu: 6, 11, 17, 18 (bottom), 22 (top), 25, 29, 32, 42; James Watt/Mo Yung Productions, 19 (top), 40; Bob Cranston/Mo Yung Productions, 22 (bottom), 34; © Peter Howorth/Mo Yung Productions, 38. Animals Animals: James Watt, 7, 13, 18 (top), 30 (top); Scott Johnson, 12 (top); Bob Cranston, 19 (center), 26, Chris McLaughlin, 33; Clay Wiseman, 37. Corbis: Jeffrey L. Rotman, 8. Innerspace Visions: © Doug Perrine, 30 (bottom).

Printed in Hong Kong

1   3   5   6   4   2

CONTENTS

1
INTRODUCING SHARKS

Sharks are sometimes called "the monsters of the deep." But although they have attacked and killed people in oceans all around the world, they are not really monsters. Most sharks aren't very dangerous to humans. Rather, many sharks are docile and shy.

Sharks live all over the world. They are found in all of the world's oceans: the Arctic, Atlantic, Pacific, and Indian. Most sharks live in warm or *temperate* waters. The whale shark and the whitetip shark live in the warm waters around the equator. Other sharks, such as some types of hammerheads, live in warm waters of the Pacific, Atlantic, and Indian Oceans. Sharks often live near the coasts of the continents. The water is usually warmer here than it is far out at sea.

Other sharks prefer colder waters. Basking sharks, salmon sharks, and Greenland sharks are found in the northern oceans. The lantern shark lives in the darkness

EVEN IF IT DID NOT HAVE THE VERTICAL STRIPES THAT GAVE IT ITS NAME, THIS SHARK WOULD PROBABLY BE CALLED TIGER FOR ITS FEROCITY AND REPUTATION AS A MAN-EATER.

CAT SHARKS ARE ONE OF THE SMALLEST TYPES OF SHARK. THERE ARE EIGHTY SPECIES, MOST OF WHICH ARE LESS THAN THREE FEET (90 CM) IN LENGTH.

of the deep ocean waters. This shark got its name because it glows in the dark.

A few sharks, such as the bull shark, live in lakes. One type of bull shark lives in a lake in Nicaragua, a country in Central America, and is known as the Lake Nicaragua shark. It has attacked and even killed people in the lake. Other sharks sometimes swim up into the mouths of rivers that empty into the ocean.

Sharks come in a range of sizes. Some sharks are enormous. The whale shark is the largest fish in the world. This shark can be more than forty feet (12 meters)

THE WHALE SHARK IS LIKE A WHALE IN SIZE, BUT ITS TAIL IS VERTICAL RATHER THAN HORIZONTAL.

long and weigh eighteen tons (16,300 kg)!

Two of the world's smallest sharks are the cat shark and the lantern shark. The cat shark is only about six inches (15 cm) long. The lantern shark is only eight inches (20 cm) long.

Because they live underwater, sharks have always been a mystery to us. Many ancient cultures, like those in New Guinea and Polynesia believed that sharks had magical powers. For this reason, they never caught or harmed sharks.

A Hawaiian legend tells about a god named Maui.

HERE IS A **FOSSIL** TOOTH FROM CARCHARODON MEGALODON (LEFT) COMPARED TO THE TOOTH OF A GREAT WHITE SHARK.

SHARKS HAVE BEEN ON EARTH FOR MORE THAN 400 MILLION YEARS. IN COMPARISON, HUMAN HISTORY IS A BRIEF MOMENT OF LESS THAN TWO MILLION YEARS. SCIENTISTS HAVE FOUND FOSSILS OF ANCIENT SHARKS. ONE OF THESE ANCIENT SHARKS IS CALLED CARCHARODON MEGALODON. IT HAD TEETH THAT WERE SIX INCHES (15 CM) LONG!

One day while he was fishing, a shark insulted him. The god threw the shark into the sky, where it can still be seen in the Milky Way. Another story about Maui says that when a shark escaped from the god's fishing hook, it swam away and became the island of Tahiti.

One of the strangest customs involving sharks was a kissing ceremony. Kissing ceremonies were performed regularly by people who lived on the islands of the Pacific Ocean. These people would go into the water and actually kiss sharks. They believed kissing would make the sharks harmless.

Ancient people also used sharks' teeth to make necklaces, bracelets, and earrings. These pieces of jewelry were often worn during religious ceremonies. Today, people can buy jewelry made of sharks' teeth in tourist shops on many beaches.

2

SHARKS OF
THE WORLD

Sharks are a kind of fish, animals having a back-bone and gills. Some fish—called bony fishes—have skeletons made of bone. Other fish have skeletons made of *cartilage*. Cartilage is the strong flexible tissue found in a person's ears and the tip of their nose. Cartilaginous fishes include the sharks and their relatives, the rays and the chimaeras.

Rays, along with skates and sawfish, are basically flattened sharks. This group includes about 470 *species*, or kinds, making it larger than the shark group. Rays range in size from four inches (10 cm) to the giant manta ray with a "wingspan"

THE BLUE SHARK IS ONE OF THE MOST COMMON OPEN OCEAN SHARKS. IT IS DARK BLUE ABOVE AND WHITE UNDERNEATH. THIS COLORING IS CALLED COUNTERSHADING AND ALLOWS THE SHARK TO BLEND IN WITH ITS ENVIRONMENT. WHEN SEEN FROM BELOW, THE WHITE BELLY BLENDS IN WITH THE LIGHTER SURFACE WATER, AND WHEN SEEN FROM ABOVE THE SHARK DISAPPEARS INTO THE DARK OCEAN BELOW.

of up to twenty-four feet (7 m). Some rays have a *venomous* spine along the tail that allows them to "sting" predators. This defense mechanism can be dangerous to humans.

The only chimaeras existing today are the rat-tails. These fish average from two to three feet (61–91 cm) in length and live at the bottom of the ocean.

THE JAWS OF A GREAT WHITE SHARK ARE TRULY AWESOME.

This brings us to the sharks. There are more than 400 species of sharks living on our planet. The most familiar shark, and the one considered to be the most dangerous, is the great white. This shark has huge jaws filled with rows of sharp teeth. These teeth can be as big as a person's hand! Great whites live in both cool and warm seas all over the world. They are fast swimmers and usually eat other fish, sea lions, and seals. However, these sharks have attacked and killed people. Off the coast of California great whites attack an average of 1.3 times per year.

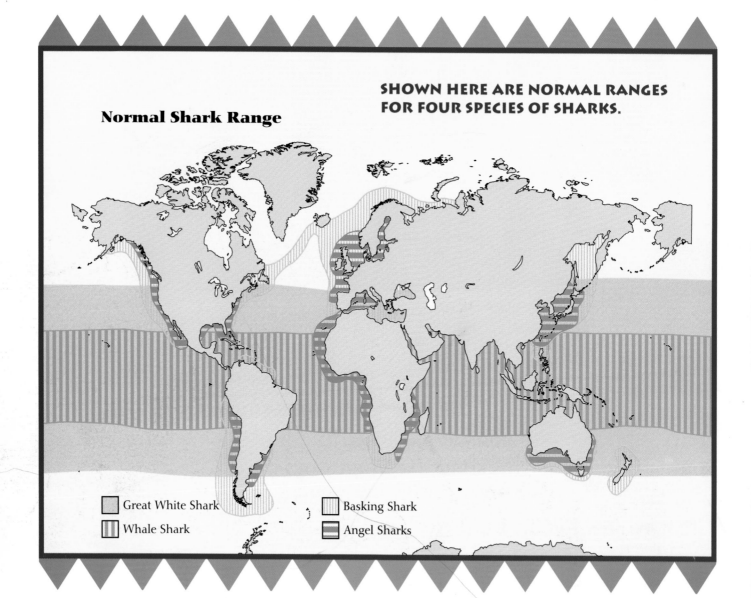

Normal Shark Range

SHOWN HERE ARE NORMAL RANGES FOR FOUR SPECIES OF SHARKS.

Great White Shark

Whale Shark

Basking Shark

Angel Sharks

Another formidable species is the hammerhead shark. One of the strangest–looking sharks, this fish has a wide, flat head like the top of a hammer. The eyes and nostrils are on the sides of its head. The position of the hammer-head's eyes lets it see things in front of and behind its body. Hammerheads eat fish, stingrays, and squid and have been responsible for attacks on humans. These sharks swim in warm, shallow waters along the coast.

THE GRAY REEF SHARK IS PRIMARILY FOUND IN THE TROPICAL AND SUB-TROPICAL WATERS OF THE PACIFIC AND INDIAN OCEANS. OFTEN FOUND AROUND CORAL ATOLLS, OR ISLANDS, AND LAGOONS NEAR OCEAN REEFS, THEY PREFER TO SWIM ALONG THE EDGES OF REEF DROP-OFFS AND IN THE SHALLOWS.

The ferocious tiger shark also has a reputation as a man-eater. It is named for the vertical stripes on its back. Tiger sharks will swallow just about anything. Scientists have found boat cushions, tin cans, wood, metal, clothing, bottles, license plates, and alarm clocks inside these sharks' stomachs. However, a tiger shark's favorite food is other fish. These dangerous fish are fierce *predators* who often eat other sharks. Tiger sharks are found all over the world in warm coastal waters.

The mako shark is one of the fiercest hunters in the animal world. A mako is the fastest shark and can reach speeds of up to twenty-five miles (40 km) an hour. Sometimes they leap high above the water. When it is feeding, a mako will swim into a school of fish, grab its *prey* in its long, sharp teeth, and swallow the fish whole.

A DIVER "HITCHES" A RIDE WITH A WHALE SHARK.

One of the slower-moving sharks is the whale shark—the largest fish in the world. This shark is very gentle and does not attack people and will actually allow divers to grab hold to its back and swim along with them. The whale shark has about 15,000 tiny teeth in its huge mouth. It swims slowly with its mouth open to catch small fish, crustaceans, and tiny organisms called *a*. These gentle giants can be found in warm waters throughout the world.

The wobbegong shark is part of a group called the carpet sharks. Their markings help them to blend in with the ocean floor, where they live. Wobbegongs rest on the bottom during the day and hunt at night for crabs, lobsters, and small fish. This shark is found near Australia, New Zealand, China, and Japan. Though considered harmless to humans, wobbegongs of Australia are known for their bulldoglike bite.

17

SHARK SPECIES

Six of the species discussed in this chapter are shown here with the average length and weight of an adult.

◀ **Great White Shark**
20 feet (6 m)
about 1,000 pounds (454 kg)

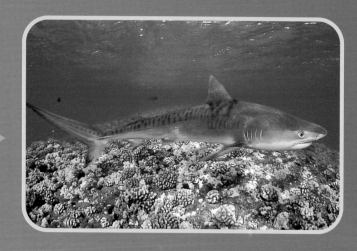

Tiger Shark ▶
10-14 feet (3-4 m)
about 1,600 pounds (700 kg)

◀ **Mako Shark**
12 feet (3.6 m)
about 1,000 pounds (454 kg)

Hammerhead Shark
20 feet (6 m)
about 1,000 pounds (454 kg)

Whale Shark
40 feet (12 meters)
18 tons (16,300 kg)

Wobbegong Shark
6-10 feet (1.83 m)
up to 300 pounds (135 kg)

19

3
THE SHARK FROM HEAD TO TAIL

A shark's body is perfectly designed for swimming. Many sharks are shaped like a torpedo—wide in the middle and narrow at either end. This design helps the shark move quickly through the water.

Sharks that live on the bottom of the ocean have flattened bodies and soft, weak tail fins. These sharks, which include angel sharks and wobbegongs, are not fast swimmers.

Most fish have a special body organ called a swim bladder. The swim bladder holds air like a balloon to keep the fish floating in the water. A shark does not have a swim bladder. Instead, its liver is filled with oil. Because oil is lighter than water, it helps keep the shark afloat. The shark

THE FEARLESS AND AGGRESSIVE OCEANIC WHITETIP SHARK, NAMED FOR ITS BROAD FINS TIPPED IN WHITE, CAN GROW TO A LENGTH OF UP TO THIRTEEN FEET (4 M).

can also live off this oil if it is unable to find food. However, a shark's oil alone is not enough to keep the animal from sinking to the bottom. Sharks must also keep swimming all the time.

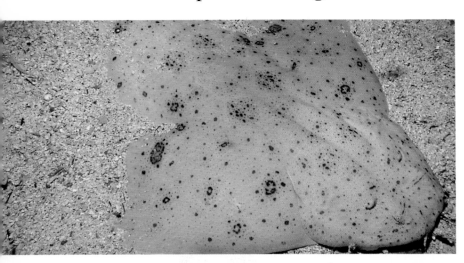

ANGEL SHARKS LIKE THIS ONE RELY ON CAMOUFLAGE TO HELP THEM CATCH PREY OR HIDE FROM PREDATORS.

THIS SHARK IS A MEMBER OF THE SIX- OR SEVEN-GILL GROUP OF SHARKS. ALL OTHER SHARKS HAVE FIVE GILLS.

A shark's constant movement also helps it to breathe. Like other fish, sharks breathe by taking oxygen out of the water as it passes through their gills. However, unlike other fish, most sharks can't pump water over their gills so they swim to keep water moving over the gills.

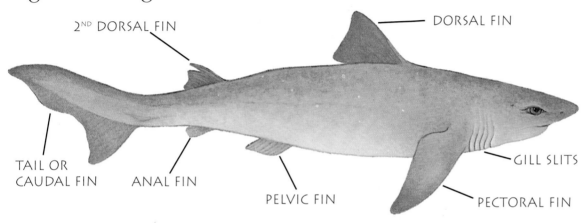

A shark's tail and fins provide lift and steering as the shark swims. Most sharks have eight fins: the dorsal fins, two fins that stick up from the shark's back; a pair of pectoral fins that stick out and down from the shark's body in the front; two pelvic fins that stick out and down from the shark's body at the back; a small anal fin underneath the shark's body in the back; and the tail, or caudal fin.

Sharks have two types of muscle tissue—red and white. Red muscle is filled with oxygen-rich blood that gives the shark energy to move for a long period of time. White muscle has a poor blood supply and sustains only short periods of movement. Whether a shark has more red or white muscle determines how well it can hunt and defend itself. The more red muscle, the stronger and faster the shark is likely to be.

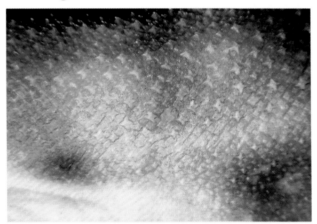

THIS CLOSE-UP OF A SHARK'S SKIN SHOWS THE DERMAL DENTICLES THAT COVER ITS BODY.

A shark's skin is very unusual. The skin is rough because it is covered with thousands of tiny toothlike structures called *dermal denticles*. Carpenters used sharkskin to smooth wood surfaces before sandpaper was invented.

A shark's teeth grow throughout its life. If a tooth breaks or falls out, another tooth moves up from the next row to take its place. Some sharks have as many as three thousand teeth in their mouth at one time. Others have only a few dozen.

A shark's teeth are arranged in rows. Usually, only the first two rows are used for biting. In time, these teeth wear out and break off or fall out and a new row of teeth moves up to take their place. Teeth can be replaced as often as every week in small sharks, and every six to twelve months in large sharks. This replacement happens continuously during the shark's lifetime.

The shape of a shark's teeth can tell you what kind of food it eats. Great white sharks eat large animals so their teeth are large and triangular and have jagged edges.

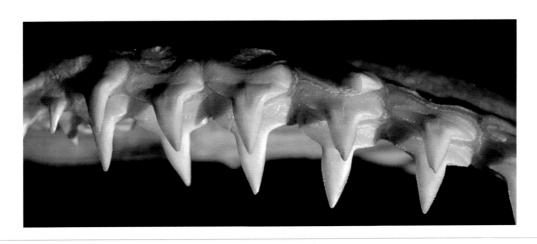

THESE ARE THE TEETH OF A BULL SHARK.

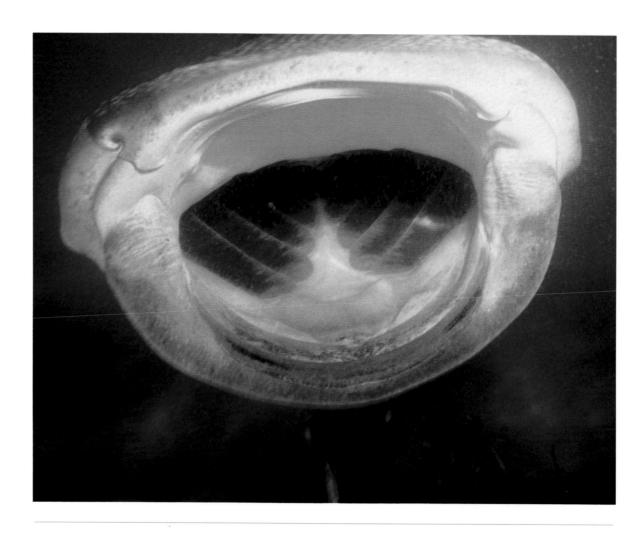

WHALE SHARKS SOMETIMES EAT WHOLE SCHOOLS OF SMALL FISH. THEY LOOK FOR SCHOOLS THAT ARE TIGHTLY BALLED UP, PERHAPS TRYING TO ESCAPE OTHER PREDATORS. WHEN A WHALE SHARK FINDS A SCHOOL OF FISH, IT RISES VERTICALLY OUT OF THE WATER TO DRAIN THE WATER VOLUME OUT OF ITS MOUTH THEN DROPS BACK INTO THE OCEAN NEXT TO THE SCHOOL. WATER AND FISH RUSH INTO THE WHALE SHARK'S MOUTH.

A mako shark catches fish with long pointed teeth and eats them whole. Other sharks, such as the wobbegong, have flat teeth to crush the hard shells of crabs and lobsters.

Filter feeders, such as the whale shark, have very small teeth. The whale shark doesn't need large teeth because it doesn't bite its prey. Instead, it eats by straining tiny plankton out of the water.

A shark's powerful jaws also help it to catch prey. The jaws are attached to a shark's skull by stretchy ligaments and muscles. These ligaments and muscles allow the upper jaw to move forward as the shark bites.

All of these special characteristics have helped sharks to survive in their underwater home for millions of years.

4
SHARK WAYS

The shark has survived as a result of successful adaptations—not only to their physical characteristics but to their habits as well.

All of the sharks' senses—and they have six of them—help them to be excellent hunters. Besides seeing well in the dim underwater light, sharks can see in color. It is also believed that they are able to see well up to 49 feet (15 m) away.

A shark's hearing is so good that it can sense a fish struggling in the water more than a mile (1.6 km) away. Sharks do not have external ears, like people do. Instead, a tiny tube carries sound waves to the inner ear inside the shark's head.

Sharks smell through two nostrils on the bottom of their snout. These nostrils are used only for smelling, not for breathing. A shark's

THE BULL SHARK CAN BE FOUND THROUGHOUT THE WORLD, OFTEN INHABITING AREAS THAT PEOPLE SHARE, SUCH AS LAKES AND RIVERS.

A SAND TIGER SHARK SWIMS AMONG A SCHOOL OF FISH OFF THE COAST OF NORTH CAROLINA.

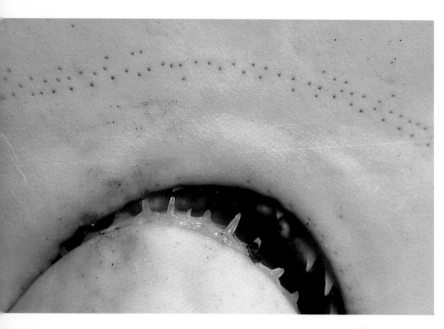

THE UNDERSIDE OF A GOLDEN HAMMERHEAD SHARK'S HEAD, SHOWING TEETH AND AMPULLAE OF LORENZINI.

sense of smell is so strong it can smell a tiny amount of blood in the water over a quarter mile (402 m) away. At one time, people called sharks "swimming noses."

A shark's sense of taste comes from pits within the mouth. Some sharks will sample items and quickly reject them. Others will eat almost anything.

Sharks also have a special sense of touch. Part of this sense is found in what is called the lateral line– a series of tiny holes that run along each side of the shark's body. These holes are connected to nerves under the shark's skin. The lateral line picks up vibrations, which the shark uses to find other animals in the water. It can sense animals more than one hundred yards (91 m) away.

In addition to the five senses of sight, hearing, smell, taste, and touch, sharks also have a sixth sense. A series of openings in the skin of a shark's head and jaws can sense the electrical impulses that other animals produce. These openings are called ampullae of Lorenzini. This ability helps the shark find prey that is buried under the sand or hidden in the darkness.

A shark's super senses help it find food. When it comes to where sharks go to look for food, there are two

different types of shark. Benthic, or bottom–dwelling, sharks swim along the bottom of the ocean. They hunt for clams, crabs, and other small animals that live on the seafloor.

Pelagic, or open–water, sharks swim through the ocean. They hunt for squid, fish, sea birds, and other animals. Some pelagic sharks are filter–feeders. They strain plankton from the water.

Sharks that eat plankton have special body parts called gill rakers in their mouths. These are long, rough strips that plankton sticks to when it floats into a shark's mouth.

Along with animal prey, some sharks have been known to eat very strange things. Scientists have found jewelry, clothes, bricks, beer cans, and other items that definitely aren't food inside sharks' stomachs. These objects end up inside sharks because these animals don't take the time to check what they are swallowing.

Luckily for the shark, its stomach has strong digestive juices that can break down almost any organic material. If a shark eats something it can't digest, it usually spits it up after a few days. Some sharks even turn their stomach wrong side out and thrust it through their mouth to get rid of indigestible objects.

There are a few animals that a shark will not eat. One of them is the porcupine fish. This fish is covered with sharp spines and can inflate its body into a spiky ball. If a shark swallows a porcupine fish, it can swell up in the shark's throat and choke it. Sharks also avoid eating poisonous animals, such

THE PORCUPINE FISH'S DEFENSE MECHANISM KEEPS IT FROM BEING PREY FOR SHARKS.

as the sea cucumber and the scorpion fish.

Because they eat so many different foods, sharks play an important role in the ocean. By eating injured, sick, or weak animals, they keep the ocean healthy for the other creatures that live there.

Sharks have also adapted ways to ensure that their offspring will survive. There are three ways that sharks reproduce. Each species has adapted the method that works best for where and how they live.

A SWELL SHARK HATCHES OUT OF AN EGG CASE.

Some sharks lay eggs. This is called *oviparous* reproduction. The eggs are covered with a tough leathery shell for protection. After a shark lays her eggs, she leaves. The eggs usually take nine to twelve months to hatch. The baby sharks can survive on their own as soon as they are born. Sharks that use this method are usually bottom dwellers.

The second type of reproduction, used by hammerheads, whale sharks, and blue sharks, is called *viviparous* reproduction. This is similar to how mammals reproduce in that the developing baby stays within the mother. From one or two to as many as fifty baby sharks, or pups, are born live and swim away. Mother sharks do not take care of their young after birth. Sharks that give birth to live young lose their appetites just before the pups are born. This keeps the mother shark from eating her own babies.

The third method of reproduction, the most common among sharks, is called *ovoviviparous*. The egg is kept within the mother's body until it develops completely. Some species, such as the spiny dogfish, have a gestation period that lasts twenty-four months. This is unusual. Most sharks give birth within twelve months.

Female sharks usually give birth to their young in the same place year after year. Male sharks never go near these birthplaces.

Baby sharks look just like their parents, only smaller. Scientists think that baby sharks can learn faster than adults. This helps them survive in the wild. Young sharks are also more aggressive than adults.

Some sharks take a long time to grow up. The larger the shark, the longer it takes. Lesser spotted dogfish are ready to mate when they are ten years old, but the larger thresher shark takes fourteen years to be fully grown. If a shark isn't caught or eaten by another predator, it can live to be thirty years old.

ALTHOUGH LARGE PREDATORS ARE NORMALLY SOLITARY CREATURES, SOME HAMMERHEADS ARE KNOWN TO GATHER IN LARGE SCHOOLS, OR GROUPS, IN SPECIFIC LOCATIONS YEAR AFTER YEAR.

5
SHARKS AND PEOPLE

Many people are afraid of sharks. They've heard news reports, read books, or seen movies where innocent swimmers or surfers are ripped to pieces by ferocious sharks. Although shark attacks do happen, they are extremely rare. There are about seventy-five shark attacks around the world every year. About two thirds of those attacks happen in the United States. You have a better chance of being struck by lightning than being attacked by a shark, and more people die from bee stings than from shark attacks.

Only three shark species are considered dangerous to people. These are the great white shark, the tiger shark, and the bull shark.

In addition to the three dangerous species of shark, about thirty other kinds of shark have been

FORTUNATELY FOR THIS KAYAKER, THE BASKING SHARK EATS ONLY PLANKTON.

known to attack humans. In many cases, these sharks were threatened or disturbed by people before they attacked. These sharks include lemon sharks, nurse sharks, wobbegongs, and sand tiger sharks.

Scientists think that many shark attacks are actually mistakes. A great white shark may think that a person paddling a surfboard looks like a sea lion swimming through the water. Since great whites eat sea lions, it isn't surprising that the shark would attack the surfer. Often, the shark will take a bite or

IN THE 1970S, THE MOVIE **JAWS** MADE THE GREAT WHITE SHARK A CELEBRITY. SO MANY GREAT WHITES WERE TAKEN BY SPORT FISHERMAN AND THRILL SEEKERS THAT THEY SOON BECAME SCARCE. THEY ARE NOW PROTECTED.

two before it realizes its victim isn't a sea lion. When this happens, the shark will usually swim away. Unfortunately for the victim, even one shark bite can kill or seriously injure a person.

Sharks also have a strong attraction to blood. If a swimmer is injured in waters where there are a lot of sharks, it is likely that these fish will come to check out the blood in the water.

HOW TO PREVENT SHARK ATTACKS

- DO NOT SWIM IN WATER WHERE SHARKS HAVE BEEN SPOTTED.
- NEVER SWIM ALONE.
- IF YOU CUT YOURSELF, GET OUT OF THE WATER RIGHT AWAY. DON'T GO BACK IN UNTIL THE CUT STOPS BLEEDING.
- SHARKS ARE ATTRACTED TO SHINY OBJECTS. TAKE OFF ANY JEWELRY BEFORE GOING IN THE WATER. IT'S BEST TO WEAR A DARK-COLORED SWIMSUIT.
- DON'T SPLASH OR MAKE WILD MOVEMENTS IN THE WATER. ACTING THIS WAY CAN ATTRACT SHARKS, BECAUSE THEY MIGHT THINK THE SPLASHING IS CAUSED BY AN INJURED ANIMAL.
- IF YOU DO SEE A SHARK, DON'T PANIC. SWIM CALMLY AND STEADILY TO SAFETY. CHANCES ARE, THE SHARK WILL NOT PAY ATTENTION TO YOU.

THREATS TO THE
ENVIRONMENT HARM
HUMANS AS WELL AS
SHARKS. IF WE CAN WORK
TO SOLVE THESE PROBLEMS,
WE WILL HELP SHARKS BY
HELPING OURSELVES.

Some beaches have used nets to keep sharks away. Surrounding a beach with nets is expensive, but it does keep out sharks. Nets have trapped hundreds of sharks, and unfortunately, because sharks can't swim backward, they cannot escape if they get caught in the nets. A trapped shark will eventually drown because it can't move enough to keep water flowing over its gills.

Although sharks have a deadly reputation, people are actually more dangerous to sharks than sharks are to us. Over the years, people have killed sharks for food. They have also used the oil in sharks' bodies to

42

make medicine, cosmetics, soap, and other items.

Millions of sharks have been killed by sport and commercial fishing. Many coastal communities hold shark–hunting tournaments. In addition to sharks that are killed on purpose, many more are caught and killed accidentally in nets put out to catch tuna.

Although people and sharks can be dangerous to each other, they can also help each other. Sharks rarely get sick, and they are able to live in polluted waters that kill other fish. Scientists have been studying sharks to see how their bodies fight disease. They hope that their research will someday help to prevent cancer and other illnesses. These strange and unusual creatures may one day be seen as life-savers, not monsters.

carnivore: an animal that eats meat

cartilage: strong, flexible tissue

dermal denticle: one of the small toothlike bumps on a shark's skin

fossil: the preserved remains of an animal or plant from many years ago

oviparous: an animal whose babies hatch from an egg laid outside of the mother's body

ovoviviparous: an animal whose babies, while still inside the mother's body, hatch from an egg and continue to grow before being born

plankton: the tiny animals and plants that float in the ocean

predator: an animal that hunts other animals for food

prey: an animal that is hunted by another animal

species: a group of animals that are all of the same kind

temperate: a climate that is not too hot or too cold

venomous: having poison

viviparous: an animal whose babies develop inside the mother's body

FIND OUT MORE

BOOKS

Banister, Keith. *Sharks and Rays*. Pleasantville, NY: Reader's Digest Association, 1995.

Cerullo, Mary M. *Sharks: Challengers of the Deep. New York:* Cobblehill Books, 1993.

Levine, Marie. *Great White Sharks*. Austin, TX: Raintree Steck–Vaughn, 1998.

Llewellyn, Claire. *The Best Book of Sharks*. New York: Kingfisher, 1999.

Palazzo–Craig, Janet. *Sharks*. Mahwah, NJ: Troll Associates, 1999.

Parker, Steve and Jane. *The Encyclopedia of Sharks*. Buffalo, NY: Firefly Books, 1999.

Robinson, Claire. *Sharks*. Des Plaines, IL: Heinemann Library, 1999.

Sanchez, Isidro. Sharks: *Voracious Hunters of the Sea*. Milwaukee: Gareth Stevens Publishers, 1996.

Sharks. New York: Golden Books, 1998.

Simon, Seymour. *Sharks*. New York: HarperCollins, 1995.

WEBSITES

AquaFacts: Sharks (Vancouver Aquarium)
http://oceanlink.island.net

The Center for Shark Research
http://www.mote.org/~rhueter/sharks/shark.phtml

Sea Life: Sharks

http://www.germantown.k12.il.us/html/shark2.html

Shark Week

http://www.discovery.com/stories/nature/sharkweek/sharkweek.html

Sharks Fearsome? (National Aquarium)

http://www.aqua.org/animals/species/sharks.html

Sharks and their Relatives (Seaworld)

http://www.seaworld.org/Sharks/pageone.html

ABOUT THE AUTHOR

Joanne Mattern has always loved animals, both wild and tame. She is the author of more than one hundred books for young people, including *Lizards* in the Animals Animals series. She lives with her husband, daughter, two cats, and a dog in New York State.

INDEX

Page numbers for illustrations are in **boldface.**